Bygone Transport
Sheffield
on the Move

Contents

First published in 2006 by: At Heart Publications 32 Stamford Street, Altrincham, Cheshire, WA14 1EY in conjunction with The Star, York Street, Sheffield, S1 1PU

Images and text: The Star (Sheffield) unless otherwise stated.

ISBN: 1-84547-100-8

Sheffield on the Move

Sheffield's development as the cauldron of British steel production in the 1800s led to a clamour for public transport. Before the days of mass car ownership, people relied on communal means to go about their business - be it to get to work, to meet their loved ones or to enjoy their leisure time.

The age of public transport was born in Sheffield in 1834 when a horse-drawn bus service running between Sheffield and Rotherham began. Four years later, Sheffield Wicker railway station opened, heralding the hissing Age of Steam.

In 1873 the first horse-pulled trams ran in Sheffield, later to be consigned to history by electric versions which rolled into action in 1899. Trams finally bowed out in 1960 when they succumbed to the greater versatility of the motor bus, which had originally come into service in 1913.

As car ownership dramatically spread, and the roads became increasingly clogged, the city's fathers looked to new ways to give people quicker access across the city. The now familiar sight of Supertram first slipped out of Meadowhall towards the city centre in 1994.

Throughout the evolution of public transport, The Star and its forerunners have been there to record history in the making. Our photographers have braved all weathers to take pictures of many of the key moments in the development of the city's transport network. These pictures, some of which have not been published before, are a tribute to their skill and dedication.

We hope you enjoy these images of the city from the depths of our photo archive as much as we cherish them.

Alan Powell
Editor, The Star

Horse Power

It's hard to imagine in these days of road rage that the worst thing people would come across on the streets of Sheffield was freshly laid horse manure.

The horse, of course, was always likely to be the first source of public transport. But as the need to travel grew – along with the increasing distances people were beginning to cover – something more was needed and the age of public transport was born.

The earliest form of public transport in South Yorkshire dates back to 1834 when a horse-drawn bus service running between Sheffield and Rotherham began. By 1873 Sheffield's horse-pulled trams appeared, operating from Lady's Bridge to Attercliffe. They proved such a success that the route was extended to Brightside and Tinsley.

Further horse tramway routes were set up to Hillsborough, Heeley and Nether Edge. The last horse clopped out of service in 1902 to be replaced by the latest technology - electric trams.

Nether Edge
terminus (© F. Hall)

Wild West? No, it's a stagecoach on Glossop Road

An early example of a horse drawn tram

On the road to
Heeley, 1886

Hansom it's not -
Fargate in the 1950s

Horse Power : Bygone Transport : Sheffield on the Move

Top hats, horses
and carriages on
Pinstone Street and
Moorhead. The
famous Roberts
department store is
in the background.

Horse and cab
admired by
onlookers during a
May Day
procession, 1906
(© Sheffield
Libraries)

Sheffield Tramways
Company on the
Attercliffe and
Tinsley route

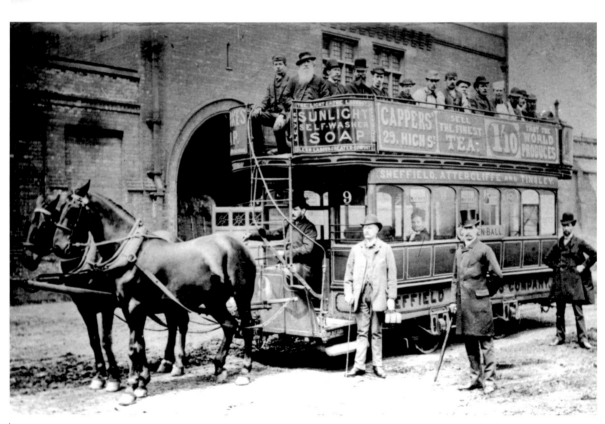

Horse Power : Bygone Transport : Sheffield on the Move

The Sharrow and
Nether Edge service

The only way to
travel in days gone by

Horse Power : Bygone Transport : Sheffield on the Move

Streets of Sheffield, 1890

Chauffeur-driven carriage during the Edwardian era

The horse-drawn tram era ended in 1902

Horse Power : Bygone Transport : Sheffield on the Move

Wells Fargo? No, it's a Sheffield Stagecoach at Hunter's Bar, 1898

Horse power meets its greatest rival, steam, at Wicker Arches

Horse Power : Bygone Transport : Sheffield on the Move

Electric Trams

The bizarre sight of steam trams huffing and puffing through the streets of Sheffield could have become reality had a trial in 1877 and 1878 proved successful. Instead it was electric trams that signalled the end of the horse.

The first electric tram route, running from Nether Edge to Tinsley, opened in 1899, and the rest of the network soon followed suit. As the demand for public transport grew, so too did the network; by 1910 it covered 39 miles of the city, and by 1951 this had increased to 48 miles.

But the rigidity of tram tracks would eventually prove their downfall. Motorbuses, which didn't need to travel on fixed routes were poised to become the champion of public transport.

Tram routes started to be abandoned and were replaced by buses from 1952. On October 8, 1960, the very last public service tram completed its journey from Leopold Street to Beauchief. Thousands of folk turned out to see a parade of 15 trams pass through the city centre for the last time. Many laid pennies on the tram tracks, which were duly bent by the trams forming a unique memento of the occasion.

Souvenir ticket for last tram journey, 1960

The tram displays:

CITY

SPECIAL

510

SHEFFIELD'S LAST TRAM

1873   1960

LAST TRAM WEEK

2ND to 8TH OCTOBER

2ND to 8TH OCTOBER

GOING... GOING... GONE

THE END OF AN ERA

THE SHEFFIELD CORPORATION TRAMWAYS

R.C. MOORE M Inst T.   GENERAL MANAGER

1873 - 1960

SHEFFIELD

TRANSPORT

Last tram week, 1960, saw a carnival of classics roll through the streets of Sheffield

The number 383 with new-era competition hot on its heels. Flat Street, 1955.

Thousands braved a wet and windy night to bid farewell

Electric Trams : Bygone Transport : Sheffield on the Move

Folk laid coins
on the tracks for
"bent penny"
mementos

DARNALL

AND INTAKE [ELM TREE]

300

Electric Trams : Bygone Transport : Sheffield on the Move

End of an era - tram
531 is resigned to
the scrapyard.
Oct 10, 1960.

PRICE 1D Sheffield Daily Telegraph

"that great organ of public opinion" - Rt. Hon. The Earl of Balfour

FOUNDED 1855

46

Millhouses terminus. A treasured memory for generations

Car 64 climbs Handsworth Hill in 1956

Electric Trams : Bygone Transport : Sheffield on the Move

A view from
Wadsley Bridge

"Soccer specials"
head for Bramall
Lane

Electric Trams : Bygone Transport : Sheffield on the Move

MIDLAND ST

VIA QUEEN

510

SHEFFIELD'S L

1873

Out in the cold
- last tram glides
into history

Electric Trams : Bygone Transport : Sheffield on the Move

An early tram amid the procession

Many of Sheffield's old beauties are now at Crich Tramway Museum

Electric Trams : Bygone Transport : Sheffield on the Move

Old splendour lovingly restored

A works' "coffin" tram brought from Bradford after the Blitz

Examples at Crich include old horse-drawn trams

Electric Trams : Bygone Transport : Sheffield on the Move

Sheffield's first
electric tram on
The Moor, Sept 5,
1899

Electric Trams : Bygone Transport : Sheffield on the Move

Number 185 to
Nether Edge at
Moorhead

The 124 climbs
Duke Street out
of the city centre

Electric Trams : Bygone Transport : Sheffield on the Move

Darnall terminus

Personal service for the lady in the front seat!

A traffic jam in Haymarket with the old GPO in the background

Electric Trams : Bygone Transport : Sheffield on the Move

Trams, LNER
goods engine and
an Austin Somerset
(centre) at Wicker
Arches, 1955

Tinsley tram
outside Chantrey
Arms, Woodseats

Electric Trams : Bygone Transport : Sheffield on the Move

Electric Trams : Bygone Transport : Sheffield on the Move

A lonely tram passes Tommy Ward's on Savile Street in 1955

Tenter Street tram depot

Electric Trams : Bygone Transport : Sheffield on the Move

Railways

In 1776, a plate railway was laid at the Duke of Norfolk's Nunnery Colliery by his estate manager, John Curr. This used L-shaped rails, and was one of the earliest examples of cast-iron railways.

The Sheffield and Rotherham Railway opened in 1838, with Sheffield's first railway station being built at the Wicker. Seven years later, the Sheffield, Ashton-under-Lyne and Manchester Railway opened the first mainline railway station in Sheffield at Bridgehouses.

In 1848 the Wicker Viaduct was opened and the first train passed over the famous Wicker Arches.

This line was extended to a new station, Sheffield Victoria Station, in 1851, and Wicker Station was replaced by Sheffield Midland Station in 1870. The Great Central Railway Line opened in 1899.

The age of steam at the Midland

A royal visit to Victoria Station in 1909

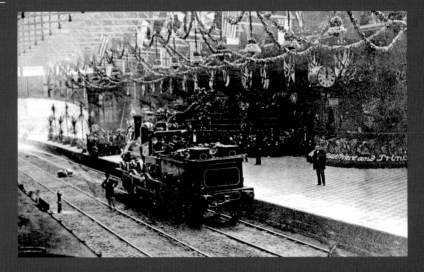

View down the platform, 1967

The Age of Steam

A 100-ton steam loco in full flight with engine roaring and whistles blazing was a sight to behold.

The thundering engines had an unforgettable appeal to scores of youngsters who would line the tracks to catch a glimpse of the metal monsters racing across the country. Trainspotting became an exciting entertainment for lads whose idea of a real thrill would be to spot a rare stream loco pass them by.

By 1968 it was all over, as diesel took over from steam. Luckily, the allure of the past age was kept alive by enthusiasts, and past glories still make nostalgic journeys along the tracks.

First SYR train to
Barnsley, 1854

Princess Margaret Rose at the Midland in 1994

A fine head of
steam at Edale,
1973

Railways : Bygone Transport : Sheffield on the Move

Duchess of Hamilton, with the Park Hill flats in the background

An old works train at Elsecar Heritage Centre

Railways : Bygone Transport : Sheffield on the Move

Sir Nigel Gresley,
1988

———————

"The Don" at work

———————

The Sheffield to
Rotherham train at
Meadowbank
(© S. Duke)

Steam engines at the pithead

George Collins of Walkley guides a car onto the train, Motorrail terminus, Sheffield, 1968

The restaurant car on the London to Harwich service in 1962

Sheffield to
Lincoln line at
Twentywell Lane,
Bradway

Railways : Bygone Transport : Sheffield on the Move

The legendary
Flying Scotsman in
Sheffield in 1969

LMR Class 5
No45101 and A3
Pacific No60102
Sir Frederick
Banbury at Victoria
Station

The Mallard
picking up speed at
Wincobank

The Mallard below
Park Hill flats, 1988

Railways : Bygone Transport : Sheffield on the Move

Victoria Station

A well-known Sheffield landmark, the Victoria, held a special place in the hearts of many. It saw the heyday of steam and was the starting point of many a family holiday to the seaside.

Victoria Station opened with a fanfare in 1851. It was hardly a grand structure, and travellers would curse the trek up a long flight of steps from the Wicker, or worse, the longer pull up Victoria Station Road to reach the ticket office.

But its dominant position on the emerging city skyline and its magnificent adjacent hotel ensured its place in Sheffield history. Sightseers as well as passengers would flock to its frontage. It was the place to be seen and the place to see dignitaries.

For many years the Royal Victoria Hotel - now the Holiday Inn Royal Victoria - held splendid balls and civic functions. Top-hatted doormen and chauffeurs were the order of the day as the Royal Vic entertained the rich and famous.

The station also created another well-known city landmark - the famous Wicker Arches, co-designed by John Fowler, who later made his name for his work on the famous Forth Bridge near Edinburgh. Although best remembered for the Golden Age of Steam, the Victoria also had an electrified line to Manchester over the Pennines.

The station was closed in 1970, although it had a brief reprieve in 1972 when work was being carried out at the Midland Station. It was eventually demolished in 1989. There was genuine sadness at its loss, and the Victoria remains high in the city's affections.

Demolition of a city landmark

The end approaching; Victoria on the brink of closure in January 1970

Station foreman, Ted Roe, with loud-hailer during the station's temporary reprieve

End of an era: Victoria Station in ruins

Midland Station

A trip to St Pancras in London starts at Sheffield Station, still known by most by its original name, the Midland Station. Today's passengers, negotiating the station's major re-modernisation programme, need vivid imaginations to picture the scene when the first train steamed away in 1870.

It opened without fanfare in the heart of grimy Sheffield, a city urgently needing better links with the rest of the country. In keeping with Victorian tradition, there were different entrances for passengers of different classes - hardly something that would be tolerated today.

With its grand Athenian architecture, the building offered passengers extensive and well-furnished facilities including the somewhat lavish first-class waiting rooms. The architecture and grand design was enough to justify it being listed as an important building where modernisation must take its splendour into account.

The station gained two extra platforms and a new facade in 1905 at a cost of £215,000. Offices were added at the north end and a large parcel office was built to the south of the main building. Two footbridges connected the platforms, one to the north for passengers and one to the south for station staff and parcel workers.

Its claim to be the gateway to Sheffield was confirmed in 1970 when all existing lines merged and operated from the Midland Station only, following the closure of both the Victoria and Bridgehouses stations.

More than 110,000 people passed through the station every week in 2005. A £35 million refurbishment programme, started at that time, aimed to make life easier for users and to give visitors a bright impression of the city.

Midland Station in
its glory days

A view of the station in 1966

Parcel staff at work, 1957

The age of steam at the Midland

Woodhead & Stations of Yesteryear

In the 1960s, controversial rail chief Dr Richard Beeching suggested a huge rationalisation programme which led to the closure of scores of small stations and rural lines.

Beeching believed the railway system should be run like a business, not a public service, and that if parts of the railway system did not pay their way — like some rural branch lines — they should be eliminated from the network.

The famous "Beeching Axe" hit the area hard in 1965 when he recommended that the Sheffield to Manchester service be consolidated. After much debate and local wrangling, British Railways favoured the Hope Valley Line, which was slower but served more local communities than its competitor.

This meant the end for passenger services along the Woodhead route and received fierce criticism from the public, eventually leading to a formal enquiry. Unfortunately, the plans were eventually approved, and on January 5, 1970, passenger services were withdrawn from the line.

This, coupled with the closure of the Great Central Railway route to London in 1966, meant that Victoria Station was ultimately rendered obsolete. But it wasn't alone, and many other small local stations were also closed as a result of Beeching's plans.

Possibly the last train on the Woodhead route before the closure in 1981

Penistone Station

BR goods yard,
Wharf Street, 1959

The electrified line
between Sheffield
and Manchester
eventually carried
freight before its
closure

1969 saw the end
of Broomhouse
Tunnel between
Sheffield and
Chesterfield

Railways : Bygone Transport : Sheffield on the Move

Lord Beeching opening Tinsley Marshalling Yards in 1965

The first all-electic train to leave Sheffield Victoria on an inaugural run to Manchester, September 1954

Beauchief Station
faced the axe in
1961

Bridgehouses
goods station lies
deserted, October
1962

Railways : Bygone Transport : Sheffield on the Move

Penistone Station,
1980

Woodhead Station,
1963

WAY OUT
PARCELS & LEFT LUGGAGE
SUBWAY TO PLATFORMS

Penistone Station, 1966

Railways : Bygone Transport : Sheffield on the Move

Class 76 electric
locos in the
scrapyard, 1983

Woodhouse
Station, 1980

Railways : Bygone Transport : Sheffield on the Move

BLANK CARDS

The ticket office,
Wortley Station

Master Cutler & City of Sheffield

There can't be many in Sheffield who have not heard of the Master Cutler train. Its journey started in 1947 when Master Cutler, the Hon R. A. Balfour, officially named the train before it departed from Victoria Station to London Marylebone.

In those days it was pulled by a steam loco - a B1 Class - finally giving way to diesel in 1958. Each of the three first-class Pullman carriages had their own kitchen and the interiors were panelled in polished mahogany. It was further updated in 1960, and in 1965 the service transferred to the Midland Station. In 1968 the train started its now familiar route from the Midland to St Pancras, known as the businessman's breakfast special.

The City of Sheffield, launched in 1944, was seen by many as it steamed along the West Coast line. It came to Sheffield only once - on the day it was unveiled. When it was scrapped, the nameplate was handed to the city and was installed in the Kelham Island Museum.

The City of Sheffield at Midland Station, November 1, 1944. Oddly, the city's most famous loco visited the city only once - on the day it was officially named. It was a LMS Coronation Class on the West Coast line operating between Euston and Glasgow.

Master Cutler, Bernard Cotton, proudly holds the famous nameplate in 1979

Sir Eric Mensforth admires his train in 1966

Driver Robert Parker at the Master Cutler controls, 1962

SHEFFIELD

The nameplate was presented to
Lord Mayor Ald J. S. Worrall in 1965
when the engine was scrapped after
covering 1,500,000 miles

The Master Cutler's
last journey to
King's Cross,
October 1968
(© L. Thomas)

Master Cutler,
Hugh Neill, receives
the new nameplate,
made by Firth Vickers
Stainless Steels Ltd
in 1959

Pulling away from Sheffield in 1962

The train was kept spick and span by an army of cleaners, 1953

A latter day Master Cutler at Sheffield in 1993

The Charabanc

The odd sight of scores of merry factory and office workers in their finery and cloth caps, whopping through the countryside in charabancs, became a familiar spectacle in the early 1900s.

Factory bosses would treat their workforce, often on bank holidays, to trips to coastal resorts and the countryside on open-top buses, or "Charras", as they were affectionately known.

At the seaside

An "ideal" way to travel

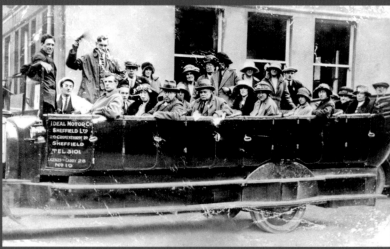

A trip to the St Leger races in 1926

Pub trip rides in style

"All aboard!" J Watt's works outing, 1919

The Works outing : Bygone Transport : Sheffield on the Move

On the Buses

Trams stayed on the tracks until 1960, but it was inevitable that motorbuses would eventually take their place as the city's number one mode of public transport.

Unhindered by the constraints of fixed tracks, their use spread rapidly from their introduction in the early 1900s.

Double and single deckers, resplendent in the Corporation's cream and navy livery, became a common sight as the city grew. The main bus station at Pond Street became a familiar destination for many at the start and end of journeys to and from town.

By the mid 1960s, the bus was the main form of public transport in Sheffield with a variety of private companies operating. In 1970, the government adopted several services to form a national bus company.

South Yorkshire Passenger Transport Executive was set up in 1974 to run services across the county and its cheap fares became a national controversy. Today a variety of public transport operators provide a network of buses across South Yorkshire.

An early single decker operated by Sheffield Corporation Motors

Barlow and Fishers,
Gilford bus

The No. 9 inner
circular service in
the early days.
The No. 138 bus
was Sheffield's
second diesel.

Sheffield Corporation Tramway's Daimler DD at Wyming Brook (© Sheffield Libraries)

The days of conductors were numbered by the introduction of pay-as-you-enter one-man buses in the 1960s

A single-decker in use for public announcements during the Second World War

On the Buses : Bygone Transport : Sheffield on the Move

Driver Mick Webber and conductress Kath Slea on Sheffield's last back loader at its retirement from service, Dec 30, 1976

The free "Bendibus" service, seen here on Pinstone Street, was popular with shoppers in the city centre

The outer circular route was much loved by children who enjoyed scenic views across the city

National Westminster Bank

Bus mayhem in
High Street in 1980

On the Buses : Bygone Transport : Sheffield on the Move

Brenda Cork
became Sheffield's
first woman bus
driver in 1976

A 1960s AEC
Regent at Sheaf
Island

On the Buses : Bygone Transport : Sheffield on the Move

The old and the new together

Articulated bus on test in Sheffield in 1977

Leyland backloader in action

On the Buses : Bygone Transport : Sheffield on the Move

GARAGE

GARAGE

GARAGE

GARAGE

2522 WE

2523 WE

2518 WE

South Yorkshire had the cheapest fares for miles around, as seen here in 1977

Double deckers on High Street, 1977

Tenter Street tram depot, pictured here in 1972, became home to buses

On the Buses : Bygone Transport : Sheffield on the Move

On the Buses : Bygone Transport : Sheffield on the Move

Pond Street bus station during the bus strike of 1968

Pond Street in 1974

Development of the Road Network : Bygone Transport : Sheffield on the Move

BATEMOOR VIA 36
GREENHILL AVENUE
BRADWAY VIA 59
GREENHILL AVENUE

NEW LIMITED
STOP JOURNEYS

HUDDERSFIELD 70 minutes
HALIFAX 90 minutes

COMMENCES In APRIL
Ask for Details

HOLMESFIELD 22
via ROCKING LANE
via GREENHILL AVENUE & STORLEY 86

DYKE VALE Rd 27

CLESALL
NGINGLOW 4

Elegant arches gave
shelter to the
length of the bus
station

The station was modernised in 1990

Buses from all over the county converged on Pond Street

Development of the Road Network : Bygone Transport : Sheffield on the Move

The upgraded Pond Street was renamed "The Transport Interchange" in 1990

Thousands of people have memories of the station which became a well-known landmark

Pond Street in front of Sheffield Hallam University with the Town Hall beyond

Development of the Road Network : Bygone Transport : Sheffield on the Move

Minitram
- the one that got away

In the 1970s, serious consideration was given to a Minitram system for Sheffield - a network of driverless electric people carriers travelling above the city streets.

The scheme was considered by the government as a solution to increasing traffic jams, but was dropped in 1975. The system - computer-controlled tramcars running from the Midland Station to the city centre - would have cost millions.

Supporters said it would have brought a revolution to transport, creating a pollution-free atmosphere.

The Minitram was proposed in 1974 and created quiet a stir

Head in the clouds... how Haymarket might have looked

If trams could fly...a Commercial Street of the future!

A mock-up of the
system serving
The Moor

Supertram

Proposals for a new tram system first appeared in the 1970s with the Minitram - a transport system which never got off the drawing board. Many years later trams made a reappearance in the form of Supertram.

After much deliberation, routes were selected and construction for the new 18-mile system, named Sheffield Supertram, started in 1991.

The first line, running from Castle Square to Meadowhall, opened on March 21, 1994. The system, which has been widely criticised by those it does not serve, runs from the city centre to Middlewood and Malin Bridge, via the University and Hillsborough, northeast to Meadowhall via Attercliffe, and southeast to Halfway and Herdings Park via Norfolk Park, Manor and Gleadless.

Supertram is operated by the Stagecoach Group under contract from the South Yorkshire Passenger Transport Executive. It is now a popular network, despite initial low passenger take-up, and there is talk of an expansion of the service.

Bus chaos during the construction phase

Supertram set new
levels of passenger
comfort

Supertram work at
Park Square
roundabout

Safe Height
13' 5"

Supertram : Bygone Transport : Sheffield on the Move

"Next stop North Pole!" - snow failed to stop the tram

Not everybody wanted to catch the tram

Thumbs up for free rides to attract passengers

Supertram : Bygone Transport : Sheffield on the Move

A driver's eye view from the cockpit

Dave Bridges was Supertram's first driver, March 21, 1994

No. 1 cuts the tape

Tram arrives by road

Supertram : Bygone Transport : Sheffield on the Move

Making easy work
of climbing Park
Grange Road

Park Square bridge
is hoisted into
place

Construction was a
major headache
and caused much
disruption in High
Street

Supertram : Bygone Transport : Sheffield on the Move

The Netherthorpe tunnel

Supertram tracks being laid on High Street. The 'cobbles' were made out of resin with fake "rust" stains added for nostalgic authenticity

Finishing work near Norfolk Park

Supertram : Bygone Transport : Sheffield on the Move

Tram lines being laid on Church Street

Development of the Road Network

It's hard to picture it now, but the first roads in the Sheffield area probably date back to the Roman occupation of Britain between 43 and 410 AD.

Long Causeway, running through Hallam, gives us a clue that getting around has always been a basic human need.

Early roads went to and from Sheffield Castle in the Middle Ages, but it was centuries later that public transport was introduced and the road system spread into something like the one we recognise today.

A turnpike from Sheffield to Chesterfield was built in 1756, and was soon followed by a toll road through Ringinglow to Chapel-en-le-Frith and Buxton in 1758. Roads to Barnsley, Tickhill, Worksop, Intake and Penistone were also constructed, and the Baslow turnpike (Abbeydale Road) opened in 1805, with Glossop Road being completed in 1821.

Pinstone Street and Leopold Street were constructed by 1879 and Fargate was widened in 1888. A modernisation plan in 1875 called for the widening of High Street, but disputes with property owners delayed this until 1895.

Work on the famous "Hole in the Road" started in 1965. It was opened in 1967, and filled in with rubble from Hyde Park Flats in 1994.

Resurfacing the growing road network, 1942

Before the jam, Rivelin Valley Road, 1981

Development of the Road Network : Bygone Transport : Sheffield on the Move

The days before
traffic jams -
Queens Road,
1968

Reginald Street

Development of the Road Network : Bygone Transport : Sheffield on the Move

Development of the Road Network : Bygone Transport : Sheffield on the Move

Park Square Island in 1991. Traffic lights were introduced to roundabouts to regulate traffic flow.

Rush hour, Sheffield
Parkway, 1982

Cars were banned
from High Street in
1973

Development of the Road Network : Bygone Transport : Sheffield on the Move

All quiet on West Street, by the long-gone Triumphal Arch in 1905

People & Transport

Where there's public transport, there are people. While transport services were set up for practical purposes, to get people to work and around town for an evening's entertainment, a strange bond has formed between the two over the years.

Most folk were saddened by the demise of steam trains and electric trams; some even forged close links with workaday diesel locos. Whenever old transport is wheeled out of retirement, a wave of nostalgia sweeps the public in droves.

We all have memories and stories connected with transport. Bus drivers are as loved by passengers as they are loathed by motorists. How many of us adored the conductor with his ticket machine - and feared the appearance of the inspector when we were trying to get a free ride?

Hundreds of enthusiasts bid farewell to the Deltics at Doncaster in 1982

People have always flocked to see a classic. Here's the Flying Scotsman in Sheffield in 1980.

The Flying Scotsman has an extraordinary appeal

The Sheffield Bus
Museum is a
popular destination

Transport draws
the crowds to
Norfolk Park, 1978

People & Transport : Bygone Transport : Sheffield on the Move

Tram drivers were proud men and their band was renowned

Generations of Sheffield children travelled to school by bus

Love 'em or loathe
'em, we all have
stories to tell about
bus drivers!

Time for tea!
Hartshead tram
drivers queue at
their canteen in the
late 1930s
(© H. Kirk)

Julie Elm and
Julie Shipman,
signal box
operators,
Shirebrook, 1985

Signs of the Times

"Don't forget to put your hand out at a request stop."

In the days when the bus was the only way to travel, all Sheffield children were taught that as they went through their own rite of passage, they also had to learn all about fare stages!

With the arrival of Supertram, all passengers had to learn how to validate their tickets before they got aboard - a complicated system said to be the blame for low passenger numbers. The city is now littered with signposts, street furniture and buildings that formed vital parts of the city's transport networks.

Supertram tickets had to be validated at tram stops when the system was introduced. Passengers complained it was too complicated and the system was eventually dropped.

City Coat of Arms at Crich

Sheffield Tramways electrical control box, now at the Crich Tramways Museum

"Supertram only" signs were erected to warn errant motorists to keep off the tracks

Plastic hazard cones became a familiar sight when street bollards were knocked down by motorists and not replaced by a hard-up council in the 1990s

Sign of the Times : Bygone Transport : Sheffield on the Move

Not a common sight - a horse and carriage stop for the city clopper

A bus stop sign in 1963...

...and how they looked by 1982

Special thanks

David H. Abdy
Arthur Allen
David John Allsop
Derek Anderson
Grace Armitage
Anthony Ashton
Ralph Aughton
Frank Bailey
Garry Baker
Margaret Bannister
F. R. Barker
Bernard Barrett
Roger Michael Battye
Rose Bell
Terry Bowman
Lewis Blades Stokes Bowring
Peter Bradshaw
Kevin Arnold Briggs
Alec Briggs
Michael Peter Brookes
Sean P. Brown
Christine Brown
Gordon Burkinshaw
Graham Butcher
Robert H. Carr
James & Henry Charlesworth
Edward & George Charlesworth
John K. Clapham
Roy Clarke
David J. Clayton
Vaughan Rowland Clough
Allan Coates
Thomas Luke Cousins
Shaun M. Cowan
Darryl Creed
Norma Crossland
M. J. Crossland
Roy Day
Philip John Depledge
J. D. Dickson
Kevin Dungworth
Malcolm Dungworth
Bobbie Dyson
Susan Eastwood
George Kenneth Edison
Roger Fidment
Robert Firth
Gareth Fleming
David Ford
Paul James Freer
Anthony Froggatt

Lee Froggatt
Clive Gardner
Martin (Matt) Giles
M. H. Glover
S. Goulding
J. W. Grafton
Mark, Amanda & Laura Graves
Harold Green
Gordon Gregory
Mr Brian Gregory
Terry Hadfield
D. P. Hague
John Hall
Robert Fredrick Hallam
Lorraine Hardy
Patrick J. Harkin
Peter Hatfield
Mark Hatfield
Mrs Kathleen Hobson
Rita Hobson
John Holmes
Stephen Howard
George Jacklin
Terry Jackson
Jason
John Joseph Kennelly
Graham John Kirk
James Larkin
Peter Latham
Amy Laycock
Levick Family
Hayley Mae Lewis
Mr Edward Lill
Raymond Keith Longden
Mr Leslie Lyngard
David Mallett
Nigel A. Marsh
John Mather
Oliver McCracken
Tony Medlicott
Mr Horrace Merrill
Audrey Moon
Brian Morrill
Niels Grundtvig Nielsen
Terry Nowlin
Norman Palmer
Dick Parrott
Malcolm Percival
Mr Christopher J. Pheasey
Phelan Family (Cork, Ireland)
Warrick Plummer

Robert Michael Prestwood
Nigel Rands
Joyce Ratcliffe
Laura Renshaw
Graham Revitt
Ray Reynolds
Fredrick Alan Rhodes
A. W. Rider
Duncan Roberts
Paul Harvey Robinson
Gerald William Roe
Dennis Rooke
Jane Rotherforth
Lynn B. Royle
Margaret Rush
Joan Schofield
Martin S. Scholey
Mr G. Searles
Anthony Shirt
Kenneth William Sidaway
Mr P. Simpson
John Skelton
Robert A. Smith
Joy South
Edwin Speight
Carolyn & Graham Spurr
Simon & Deborah Spurr
Graham Tasker
John N. Taylor
Jean Mary Taylor
Brian Thompson
Alan Thornton
Tony
Stuart M. Trotter
Ray Wagstaffe
Stephen Wainwright
Geoffrey L. Ward
Stephen Ward
Ada Watson
Paul Watson
William Norman Webster
Doreen Webster
Samuel White
Mr Robert Whitham
Patrick T. Widdowson
Raymond Wilde
Leonard Wilkinson
Ela Yalcin
Trevor Yeardley
Terry Young